How to Handle Cyberbullying

UNDER PRESSURE

How to Handle Cyberbullying

by Honor Head

A+

Smart Apple Media

Published in 2015 in the United States by Smart Apple Media, an imprint of Black Rabbit Books

Smart Apple Media
PO Box 3263, Mankato, Minnesota 56002

Copyright © Arcturus Holdings Limited

The right of Honor Head to be identified as the author of this work has been asserted by her in accordance with the Copyright, Designs and Patents Act 1988.

Editors: Rachel Minay and Joe Harris
Design: Emma Randall
Cover design: Emma Randall

Picture Credits
Shutterstock: cover (antart; Igor Klimov; Sascha Burkard; scyther5), 3 (BrianWancho), 6 (Huntstock. com), 7 (Andrey Shadrin), 8 (oliveromg), 9 (Monkey Business Images), 10 (Sylvie Bouchard), 11 (Monkey Business Images), 12 (CREATISTA), 13 (William Perugini), 14 (John Blanton), 15 (nenetus), 16 (wavebreakmedia), 17 (Diego Cervo), 18 (OLJ Studio), 19 (Rob Marmion), 20 (David Stuart Productions), 21 (absolute-india), 22 (Christo), 23 (Monkey Business Images), 24 (wavebreakmedia), 25 (Liliya Kulianionak), 26 (Samuel Borges Photography), 27 (Sergey Peterman), 28 (Lucky Business), 29 (Michael Chamberlin), 30 (Eugenia-Petrenko), 31 (Monkey Business Images), 32 (Andrew Lundquist), 33 (alephcomo), 32 (Subbotina Anna), 35 (Monkey Business Images), 36 (Aleksei Semjonov), 37 (Olga Reutska), 38 (Samuel Borges Photography), 39 (Forster Forest), 40 (Syaheir Azizan), 41 (Monkey Business Images), 42 (RimDream), 43 (Monkey Business Images).

Library of Congress Cataloging-in-Publication Data

Head, Honor.
 How to handle cyberbullying / Honor Head.
    pages cm. -- (Under pressure)
Includes index.
Audience: Grade 7 to 8.
 ISBN 978-1-59920-826-8
1. Cyberbullying--Juvenile literature. 2. Internet--Moral and ethical aspects--Juvenile literature. I. Title.
 HV6773.15.C92H43 2015
 302.34'302854678--dc23
                                            2013047543

Printed in China

SL003659US
Supplier 29, Date 0514, Print Run 3391

987654321

CONTENTS

WHAT IS CYBERBULLYING?

Cyberbullying is a kind of cruel behavior that makes use of digital equipment, such as cell phones, computers, and tablets. Cyberbullies use text messages, social networking sites, instant messaging (IM) services, emails, and chat rooms to deliberately and repeatedly upset, embarrass, **humiliate,** or threaten people. Cyberbullying can also include setting up fake accounts to use against someone.

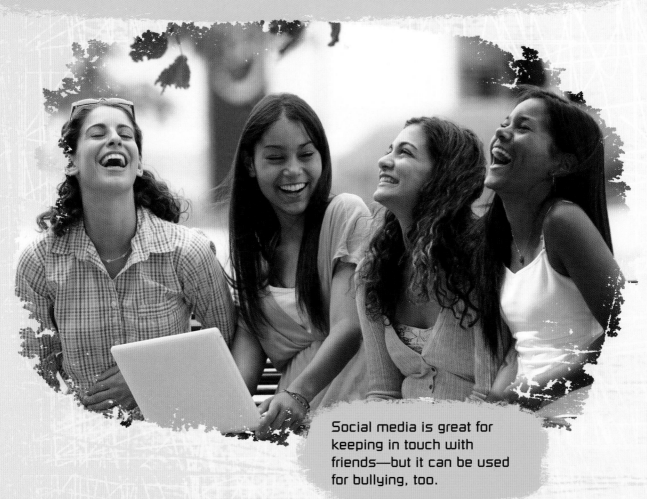

Social media is great for keeping in touch with friends—but it can be used for bullying, too.

ACTIVE ONLINE BULLYING
Cyberbullying can involve actively targeting a person. It can involve sending mean text messages or emails, starting untrue chat room rumors, and posting embarrassing photos or information on networking sites.

LEFT OUT

Cyberbullying can also mean ignoring someone's posts, texts, and emails, avoiding him or her in an online game, or blocking someone on a social network. Bullies do this in order to make that person feel isolated, alone, and a loser.

ONE OR MORE

Cyberbullying can be carried out by one person or a group. Some cyberbullying is an extension of real-life bullying, but in many cases, the target won't know who the bully is.

"New school, new friends"

I started a new school in the middle of a semester and found it hard to make friends. No one seemed to want to get to know me. Then I started getting these messages on my cell saying I was not wanted at the school, I should go away, and other really horrible stuff. I'm not sure how they got my number—I must have left my phone lying around. I told my best friend from my old school, and he said to change my cell phone number, which was really easy to do when I told the **provider** I was being bullied. We also started going to a skatepark together after school. There were a few kids there from my new school. We started to talk—now I've made some new friends, and I don't get nasty calls anymore. I think the bullies have given up on me.

Cyberbullies can target anyone, anywhere, via cells or computers.

HOW IS CYBERBULLYING DIFFERENT?

Cyberbullying is different from other forms of bullying. Cyberbullies can remain **anonymous**—and not having to face their target makes it easier for some people to behave in a cruel way. Cyberbullying can happen anywhere and at any time, and it often spreads very fast. It can make the target feel isolated and scared.

Not knowing who is sending nasty messages can make the target feel even more helpless.

INVISIBLE BULLY

Bullying is easier in cyberspace. People who wouldn't bully someone face to face might do it online, because they don't have to face their target and their target usually won't know who they are.

FALSE IDENTITY

A person who wants to bully others online can use a false **identity**. Someone who wants to be thought of as nice and friendly can secretly bully people online without anyone else knowing. This makes the bully feel safe. However, he or she can still be traced by someone with the right equipment.

Even home no longer feels safe for someone being cyberbullied.

Under Pressure Q&A

NO SAFE PLACE

Cyberbullying is very distressing for the target because it can happen anywhere. Nowhere feels safe because the bullying can even follow the target into his or her own home. The victim's phone or computer—an important link to his or her friends and social life—now becomes something they will dread.

RAPID SHARING

A nasty message or photo can spread rapidly online. It can be shared and reposted so that it reaches hundreds or even thousands of people in a short period of time. Many posts, such as photos, can be online for years to come.

Will she share my embarrassing pictures?

My ex-best friend has lots of pictures of me doing silly things. I'm not naked or anything, but they are very embarrassing. What can I do to make sure she doesn't send them to everyone?

Talk to her and ask her to respect your privacy. You don't say why you're not friends anymore, but if you were friends once, I would hope she would not share them with everyone. Are there other people in the pictures? If so, perhaps they could talk to her as well—she might listen to other people. If she does send the pictures, the best thing to do is ignore them and her. They will soon be forgotten.

WHO GETS CYBERBULLIED?

Anyone can become a victim of cyberbullying. The Cyberbullying Research Center found that up to 20 percent of young people have reported an experience of cyberbullying at some time. Young people who are bullied face to face at school often become online targets, too. Some people are deliberately targeted; some might be targeted because of a misunderstanding, or a game that gets out of hand.

It is shocking to receive a mean message or photo. If it keeps happening to you, you must take steps to stop it quickly.

ANYONE CAN BE TARGETED

It is likely that every student at your school uses social media and cell phones to stay in touch and find out what's going on—so any one of these people could be a target for cyberbullies. Even someone who doesn't have an online presence can still be a target for cyberbullies. For instance, a photo of him or her could be uploaded by someone else and circulated with nasty comments or **Photoshopped** to look embarrassing.

Everyone laughing at a photo of someone might be really embarrassing and hurtful for that person.

MISUNDERSTANDINGS

People often sound more aggressive online than they realize. It is easy to send a message that is misunderstood, because others can't hear the voice or see the face or body language of the sender. If someone thinks you have sent a nasty message and you didn't mean to, say so right away and apologize. Otherwise, you may be seen as a bully or become a target of bullies yourself.

NOT FUNNY!

Cyberbullying can sometimes start as a game that gets out of hand. For example, a game asking your friends to rate each other's pictures online might seem fun at first, but it could quickly lead to nasty name calling about some pictures and one photo or person being targeted.

"It was scary how quickly it happened"

I sent what was supposed to be a private joke to a few of my friends about another girl in our class. It was mean and I shouldn't have said it, but it was never meant for her to see. But one of my friends must have forwarded it to some other people because the girl found out. She really turned on me and accused me of being mean and a bully. Before I knew it, lots of people at school started to send me hate mail. It was horrible. She wouldn't talk to me, so I wrote her a note and said I was sorry and asked if we could talk. She agreed, and I apologized again and told her I should never have sent the message in the first place. We get along now and all the mean messages have stopped, but it was scary how quickly it happened.

WHO BECOMES A CYBERBULLY?

Anyone can be a cyberbully. Some people deliberately set out to bully and hurt another person; others may fall into it almost without realizing it—or by just going along with what their friends are doing.

POWER

Some young people bully others because hurting someone else makes them feel powerful, or because they are showing off in front of their friends. Young people who bully others at school may extend that abuse to online bullying because they want to cause as much pain and distress as possible.

FANTASY GAME

Some young people who would never bully someone to his or her face become cyberbullies. This is because they don't see the hurt they cause their victim, and it can almost feel as though they're playing a fantasy game. This type of cyberbully may not stop and think about the misery they may be causing.

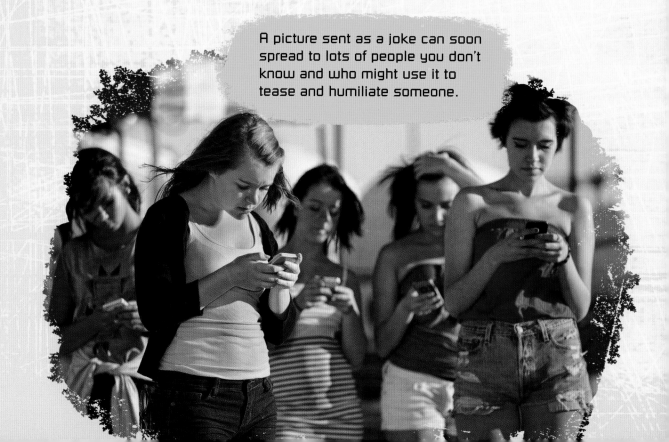

A picture sent as a joke can soon spread to lots of people you don't know and who might use it to tease and humiliate someone.

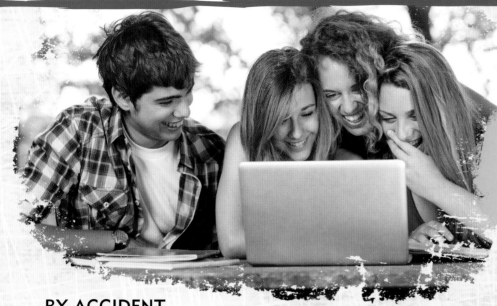

Even if someone laughs along with others at embarrassing photos or messages, deep down, it could be really hurting them.

BY ACCIDENT

You could have been part of cyberbullying without meaning to. Maybe you've made a rude comment about someone's picture or a post they've made. Maybe you thought it was just funny and no one would get hurt, but people do. Even if the person laughed along with you, he or she could still be very upset.

THINK BEFORE YOU CLICK

It can be easy to make a comment online that starts a thread of mean responses. For example, it could be a comment about how someone looks or what they're wearing. If you're making any personal comments, read them carefully before you post them. Would you be happy if someone made the same comment about you?

Under Pressure Q&A

I feel really bad—what should I do?

I may have started off a thread of nasty messages to someone by mistake. A girl sent us a picture of her and her friends, and I said something rude about one of them. It was supposed to be a joke —I didn't think everyone would see it. But someone resent the photo, and now everyone's adding to the rude comment I made. I don't know the girl well, but I feel really bad. What should I do?

First, speak to the girl and apologize—just knowing it wasn't done deliberately to hurt or bully her will help. Post a message asking people to stop showing the photo and say that the nasty comments have to stop.

TEXTS AND CELL PHONE BULLYING

Cell phones can be used to send nasty text messages or to make frightening and threatening calls at any time of the day or night. The target could receive these calls or texts when he or she is at school, at home, or even on vacation. If this is happening to you, don't worry—there are ways to deal with it.

DON'T RESPOND

Cell phone bullying can include insulting or threatening texts, nasty verbal messages, sending humiliating photos, or even silence—when you answer, no one speaks. It is a natural reaction to want to respond to bullying messages, to tell the sender to stop or go away—or just to be nasty back—but don't. This is what the bully wants, so don't give him or her the satisfaction.

TEXT WARS

Some people become targets for text wars. This is when a gang of bullies get together and send thousands of texts to one person. This can be very frightening for the victim.

Cell phones are essential to stay in touch, but they also mean a bully can reach you anywhere, at any time.

Only share your cell phone number with people you trust not to pass it on without your permission.

NOT ALONE

If you experience this kind of bullying, you may feel that you are completely alone. However, there are many places that you can turn for help and advice. You can speak to a trusted adult, such as a parent or youth leader. Your cell phone provider will provide an advice helpline. And if you think that people at your school could be involved, you should speak to a teacher.

HARASSMENT AND THE POLICE

Sending someone threatening messages is a form of **harassment**, which is illegal. If you are sent threatening messages—and especially if the sender is a grown-up—you should speak to a trusted adult about contacting the police.

"I started getting calls in the middle of the night"

I suddenly started getting calls on my cell phone in the middle of the night. When I answered, no one responded—or I could hear laughing or heavy breathing. It kept happening for about a week, and I was getting so tired at school. Then I simply turned my cell off at night. I'm sleeping OK now, but it's still weird to know someone might be trying to get through to me.

RECORD, REPORT, BLOCK

If you're getting nasty texts or voice messages on your cell, follow these simple rules. Save all text and voice messages as evidence. Report the bullying to your school and the phone provider, and block the number. If you are scared about your safety, you could speak to an adult about contacting the police.

If you are receiving nasty messages out of school hours at home, and you know they are coming from someone who goes to your school, you should report it to a teacher.

STORE AND IGNORE

Try not to delete the bullying text messages, calls, pictures, or videos—this will be your first reaction, and it's very natural, but you should save them as evidence. However, you do not have to read every text. If you recognize the bully's number, you can store a message without reading or listening to it.

DATE AND TIME

Keep a note of the date and time when you get bullying calls. If you can, try to listen for any background noise that might provide clues about where the caller is. Is it just one person, or does it sound as though it might be more than one? You can mention this when you report the bullying.

CALL THE HELPDESK

Most cell phone providers have a helpdesk to advise you on how to deal with **abusive** calls. They won't judge you or think you are being silly or that it's your fault—they are there to help. Alternatively, you could go online to see what safety and antibullying **procedures** they have.

Cell phone and social network providers will do what they can to help if you are being cyberbullied.

BLOCK THE BULLIES

Your cell phone provider will be able to block the number or numbers of the bullying calls. They will also give you the option to change your own number. You may need to replace your SIM card, and some providers will give you a free replacement card if you are being bullied. If you change your number, you will be able to give it to just your trusted friends.

Under Pressure Q&A

How can I stop the nasty calls?

I am getting some really creepy phone calls. When I answer the phone, I hear a lot of voices saying nasty things, really abusive stuff. It's making me very frightened. I feel too ashamed to tell anybody as it's so upsetting. I can't handle much more. How can I make it stop?

I'm really sorry you are going through this. It sounds like a group has gotten together to send you nasty calls. If you know the numbers these calls come from, don't listen to them in the future, but save them as evidence. Try and make a note of the dates and times you receive the calls. Contact your cell provider, explain what is happening, and ask them to block these numbers or to give you a new number. They may also try and trace the number the calls are coming from. You should tell an adult about this.

EMAILS

Cyberbullies can send emails that include mean messages, humiliating photos, or other material intended to upset or offend you. As with bullying texts, you should never reply to them, but store them as evidence and then report them to your internet service provider (ISP).

NEVER REPLY

If you receive emails that contain nasty messages or photographs, don't reply. The bully cannot get much satisfaction if he or she is unsure whether you have received or read them. Hopefully, the bully will get bored and stop, but if it goes on, tell an adult and save or print the emails to show as evidence.

FALSE ACCOUNT

Some bullies create a false email account to keep their identity a secret. You should be able to block unwanted emails, but how you do so will vary with each internet service provider. Contact your ISP via their website or by phone, tell them what's happening, and ask how you can block bullying emails.

Search online or check with your ISP to find out how to block emails from cyberbullies.

Check the subject bar and address quickly before opening emails. Do not open any that seem strange or suspicious.

VIRUS WATCH

Some emails contain **viruses** or other **malicious** software that can damage your computer. Never reply to emails if you do not know who they are from, as they could be sent by someone trying to deliberately attack your computer or trying to get into your computer to steal your personal information. Never open attachments unless you know who they're from and what's inside them.

"It was her all along"

I made friends with a girl at school, and I confided in her about some problems I was having with my now ex-boyfriend. We swapped email addresses, and soon after, I started receiving some really nasty emails from other people at my school making fun of the problems I'd had with my boyfriend. I thought he must have told someone, and we had a huge fight. I looked for my friend and found her laughing at the latest email she'd sent me with a bunch of other girls. I was so shocked—it was her all along. I closed down my online accounts and started hanging out with some different friends who go to my dance class. I don't talk to her now, but the bullying has stopped—and I won't hand out my email address to just anybody in the future.

SOCIAL NETWORKING AND CHAT ROOMS

Social networking sites and chat rooms are both great ways to keep in touch with friends online. However, they are also places where it is easy for cyberbullies to post upsetting messages and photos.

There are lots of social networking sites—check which ones have high privacy and safety ratings before you sign up.

DON'T ASK WHY

Some cyberbullies are strangers who deliberately say nasty things online to cause trouble. People like this are called "trolls." Sometimes trolls gang up against one person and can make his or her life miserable. If nasty, untrue, or personal messages are being posted about you that are upsetting or humiliating, don't respond. There is no point in asking the bully why he or she is being nasty or what you've done wrong. You haven't done anything wrong—the bully just enjoys being mean.

GET EVIDENCE

If you are being bullied via a social networking site, see if the site has a "report abuse" button you can press. Keep **screenshots** of the abuse and any other details that might be useful for when you report it. You can click on the bully's name to block or ignore his or her messages. Check out the site's preferences and privacy settings to restrict who is able to contact you in the future.

Under Pressure Q&A

Have I made things worse?

I started chatting online to someone from another grade in my school who I thought was really nice—we seemed to have a lot in common. Now she is saying really nasty things about me that are all lies—she doesn't even really know me. I challenged her and asked her why she was being so horrible—this started lots of new posts from her telling me not to be such a baby, that I deserved it, and other really mean things. I seem to have made things worse—what should I do?

It is never a good idea to respond to cyberbullies. You should walk away from this chat room and take a digital break for a little while. Think about trying a new hobby or going out with your friends. If you do go back onto the same chat site, use a different name.

CHAT ROOMS

What you say in a chat room is read by others instantly, so read your own posts through carefully and think before you click. It is easy to send something personal or even rude without realizing it, and if this happens, you might be branded as a cyberbully. So think before you send.

If you become the target of a chat room bully, don't get into a war of words. Leave and join another chat room, or better yet, do something offline.

21

INSTANT MESSAGING

Instant messaging (IM) is a great way to chat with friends and find out what is going on. However, cyberbullies can target people through IM. They might steal other users' passwords and misuse their accounts; or they might post upsetting material or cruel gossip. Choose an IM provider that has good safety procedures.

If someone is sending you nasty messages, click on their name to try and find out who they are, or look for the Help button and follow instructions.

SAFE CHAT

There are some simple steps you can follow to keep online chat safe. Choose an IM provider that has "ignore" or "block" buttons, easy ways to report bad behavior, ways to save messages for evidence if you need to, and ways to block messages that come from people who are not on your buddy or contacts list.

MISUSING YOUR ACCOUNT

Some people bully others by taking over their IM or social networking accounts. This can happen if the victim forgets to log out of his or her account, or if he or she doesn't have a cell phone lock. It can also be the result of **hacking**. The bully then sends out abusive messages from that person's account, which leaves the victim isolated and being accused of bullying. If someone uses your account in this way, change your password, and report it to the site provider immediately.

Share your worries with your friends. They can help you report online bullying or contact the helpdesk for advice for you.

CHANGE YOUR NAME

If people you know from school or outside start to bully you online, change your IM user name and only tell your new name to those you really trust. Better still, take a break from instant messaging and do other things offline.

Under Pressure Q&A

"I was angry—how can I make things right?"

I did something really stupid. Someone posted a message that made me angry. I sent a response without thinking—and I got a lot of messages in return telling me that I was behaving like a bully and that I should respect other people's opinions. I hate it that people think I'm some kind of terrible bully. How can I fix this?

Digital media make it so easy to fire back responses without thinking—it's all about that situation of not seeing the other person and so not moderating what you say as you would in real life. So, next time you feel very strongly about something, take a few deep breaths, count to 50 or do whatever you need to, and calm down before you respond. It's also a good idea to check your response before you send it—it is easy to make mistakes and say something you don't mean when you are feeling angry or stressed.

23

BASICS TO STAY SAFE

There are several basic safety measures you can take to make life as difficult as possible for cyberbullies. Always be careful about what you post online, use the highest privacy settings, and keep your password safe.

ONLINE FOR YEARS

Never forget that what you put online says a lot about you and who you are. Even if you delete a file or message on your sites, once it's out there, you can't control where it goes. Also, what is posted online now may even affect your job opportunities in the future, since employers often review online profiles of people they are considering for a job.

PRIVACY SETTINGS

When you set up a profile, always make sure you mark it as private—make this a priority when you set up the profile, and check with the site's instructions that you have the maximum amount of privacy possible. You shouldn't use a site that doesn't have a privacy setting. Otherwise, anyone who goes to your profile can copy your photos or information. Being private could save you from bullying and malicious online users.

Be careful about using computers in public places, such as coffee shops, where passwords can be easily stolen. Never access your online bank account or other sensitive information on a shared computer.

To create a strong password, make it a mix of letters and numbers, using lower case and capital letters. Never use something very obvious, such as your address or a pet's name.

KEEP PASSWORDS SAFE

Keep your passwords safe—don't share them with anyone, not even your best friends. If you think someone has found out your password, change it right away. It's a good idea to change passwords regularly, anyway.

"I took a digital break"

I was being cyberbullied on my cell phone and on my computer. I found out who was doing it and did everything I could to put a stop to it. But I couldn't stop thinking about what the bully was doing or saying—it was taking over my whole life. My teacher suggested I close down all my accounts and stay offline for a little while. I was horrified—I hated being bullied, but being online was the best way I had of keeping in touch with my friends. But actually, it turned out to be a really good thing. I explained what was happening to my friends, and we started to plan stuff in advance—if someone changed their plans, they called me on my landline and left a message. My dad got me a secondhand bike, and now I've joined a local cycling group. It's really cool. I'm back on my cell phone now and the bullying has stopped, but I didn't miss it as much as I thought. I would recommend a digital break to anyone.

PHOTOS AND VIDEOS

Deliberately posting personal photos and videos with the intent to humiliate or upset someone is a form of cyberbullying. Photos and videos can very quickly be shared around a whole school—or even go **viral**.

KEEP PRIVATE PHOTOS PRIVATE

Fun photos showing you goofing around with your friends or special photos of you and your girlfriend or boyfriend may be very personal, but once they are online, they can easily be shared with thousands of other people. To make sure that your most personal photos stay private, keep them offline.

NO CONTROL

You may think taking a photo of yourself at home to send to your best friend, boyfriend, or girlfriend is just between you and the other person, but your friend may send it on to someone else, and that person may send it to another friend, and someone along the line might decide to use it to tease or humiliate you. A cyberbully could send that very private photo of you to everyone in the school.

It's fun taking photos of you and your best friend, but once a photo is online, it is not under your control anymore.

If a nasty photo or video of you has been uploaded, tell an adult you trust, and find out the best way to remove it.

BLOCK OR DELETE

YouTube, Twitter, and Facebook have ways to block or delete particularly nasty videos or photos, so get in touch with them if something is circulating that shouldn't be out there. But they won't do much if the picture is just embarrassing.

SEXTING

Sexting is sending a naked or a nearly naked photo of someone or a sexually explicit message via cell phone. If someone is sending you photos like this that are upsetting you, report it to an adult right away. If someone asks you to send some photos of yourself like this, refuse, no matter how well you know them. You could really regret it.

"I was horrified by my photo"

I was being bullied at school—name calling and that type of thing. One day, a group of classmates stopped me and took my photo without my permission. Later, I saw the photo online—I was horrified. They had Photoshopped it so that it looked as if I was doing something really gross. The bullies sent it to everyone in the school. I was so ashamed. A teacher saw it, and I was sent to see the school counselor. I told her what had happened, and she understood. She said I should have spoken to her sooner about being bullied. The school took the photo off all the websites they could, but I know it is still out there.

PRETENDING TO BE YOU

One particularly nasty form of cyberbullying is when a bully sets up an online profile pretending to be the person they are targeting. The bully then does a lot of things that are embarrassing or mean in the name of the person they are pretending to be.

PERSONAL INFORMATION

Some cyberbullies create an account with a social networking site or chat room using someone else's photo and personal information. This can be very dangerous if they include a home or school address since it could make the person the target of online **predators**.

FALSE ACCOUNT

Once a false account has been set up, the bully can start using the site to make remarks that are offensive, rude, or even illegal in the other person's name. They can also put up offensive photos or videos—again, all in the other person's name.

Always log out correctly before you leave your computer, so that no one can steal your password or other personal information.

BULLY BLOG

The cyberbully could start a website or blog deliberately to harm their target. He or she might share **confidential** information about the target and upload photos that were intended for private use only. If this happens to you, keep a copy of the posts and report the site to the service provider immediately. If you think the bully might be from your school, you should tell a teacher.

"The messages weren't from me"

I had no idea someone was sending messages in my name until a few people at school started giving me funny looks and turning their backs on me. Then a couple of friends asked why I was sending out these messages saying cruel and abusive things about people in my class—even my friends! A teacher found out about the messages, and I had to go and see him, but luckily, he believed me when I said they weren't from me. I had no idea who was doing it, but we figured out it must be someone from the school—I was always leaving my phone lying around. The teacher made an announcement about the messages to my class at an assembly, and they suddenly stopped. We might never know who was responsible, but I'm going to keep a better eye on my phone in the future.

You could speak to a teacher about having a special assembly about cyberbullying.

HATE CAMPAIGNS

Some cyberbullies might start an online hate **campaign** that could include setting up an online poll or flooding the target with messages or images. Most hate campaigns take place over a period of time and can get more and more vicious. Sometimes they might start off as a "joke" that quickly turns nasty.

Simply by looking at an embarrassing or abusive photo or message—and not doing anything to stop it—you are encouraging cyberbullying.

OTHERS JOIN IN

It is easy for a bully to start an online hate campaign by getting others to support what they're saying. This can result in lots of mean comments aimed at one person. Many people who would never see themselves as cyberbullies might join in because "it's just a joke," and they don't realize the distress they're causing.

If you are the target of a hate campaign, get in touch with your service provider and tell them what's happening.

SWITCH OFF

If you are being cyberbullied in this way, switch off your phone or computer and tell an adult you trust. Ask him or her to help you deal with it, so that you don't have to see the hateful messages or pictures. Do not suffer in silence, think it's nothing, or that it will just go away—if it's making you upset or angry, it cannot be allowed to continue.

DON'T TAKE PART

Don't take part in cyberbullying by joining a campaign like this. Think before you "Like" a post or photo that might upset someone, and don't forward or repost a nasty message, video, or photo—that makes you a bully, too.

"My picture's out there forever"

I sent my boyfriend a silly photo of me that was only supposed to be for him to see. We recently split up, and now I've heard that he's sent it to everyone in the school. All my friends are reposting it and passing it around, even though I've asked them not to. They say it's funny and that I'm being too sensitive, but it's really embarrassing me, and I can't stand the thought of my mom or dad seeing it. I know there's nothing I can do about it, and it makes me feel sick to think the picture will be out there forever. I'll never do anything like that again.

ON YOUR OWN

Being ignored in chat rooms, online games, IM, or social networking sites is a form of cyberbullying that can be very hurtful. For most young people, their social life is planned online—without it, they may not know what's going on where or when. Being isolated digitally can make a person feel friendless and worthless.

ISOLATED AND IGNORED

Cyberbullying by excluding or isolating someone includes dropping that person as a "friend" or contact, ignoring him or her online, or refusing to play online games with him or her.

DEPRESSED

If a group gets together and decides to exclude someone from online activities, this can make the target feel as if the whole world is ganging up against him or her. It is just as bad as being left out at school. It can lead to low **self-esteem**, **depression**, and harmful behavior.

Being left out of online social activities can be very distressing. Don't let this happen to someone you know.

AN OFFLINE LIFE

If this form of cyberbullying is happening to you, one positive approach is to see this as an opportunity to build another life offline. Look around for some clubs you can join, or find a new group of friends at school. If you're not online, nothing the cyberbullies do or say (or don't do or say) can hurt you.

SAY HELLO

If you know someone who is being left out online, try to talk with them if you see them sitting alone in the lunchroom or during a break. Give him or her a smile or say hello—just knowing he or she is not totally alone will really mean a lot.

"A real life!"

Like most of my friends, I spent a lot of time online, especially playing games. Then for a really stupid reason—something to do with tactics in an online game—all my friends turned against me and stopped playing online with me. Then they stopped letting me know what they were up to and where they were going. At first, I felt really bad and didn't know what to do with myself, but then I decided to take up a real-life sport. I found a fantastic martial arts group not far from me and have been going there twice a week for about four months. I've made some great new friends, and I'm really enjoying it. So, thanks to the bullies for giving me the chance to get a real life offline.

Beat the bullies and get a life offline—you might even discover a hobby or sport you really like.

33

HACKING AND VIRUSES

Hacking and spreading viruses are particularly vicious forms of **antisocial** online behavior. Hackers and virus programmers are like bullies, but they do not care who they hurt, and they can cause serious damage to your computer that could cost a lot of money to correct.

VIRUSES AND WORMS

Viruses and **worms** are spread from computer to computer through shared messages and files. They can also be targeted to individual people. In extreme cases, they can be sent by cyberbullies. Some viruses and worms can cause little things to go wrong, so your computer doesn't operate as well as it should; others can cause a lot of damage.

TROJAN HORSE

A Trojan horse or Trojan is a piece of **malware** that can be very harmful to your computer. It attaches itself to your computer and can really mess it up. To keep your computer safe, never download software from people you don't know or trust, never open email attachments that you don't recognize, and only download games from well-known and safe sources.

HACKERS

Hackers can get into other people's online accounts to see what they're doing. Once they're in, they can steal things such as passwords and personal photos. They may use this information to steal money or cyberbully their victims.

Hackers are skilled users who know how to break into personal online accounts and steal private information.

Ask an adult to help you report that your account has been hacked.

IF IN DOUBT, DON'T OPEN IT!

The best way to stop viruses and hackers is to invest in good **firewall** and antivirus software. But in general, be careful that you don't open unknown files or emails, or click on unwanted pop-ups or attachments. If you have any doubt, delete a message without opening it.

Under Pressure Q&A

Should I open the emails?

I have been cyberbullied for about a month now—I keep getting silent calls, and then I get really nasty text messages and emails. Now I am getting lots of emails sent to me from addresses I don't know. I think a lot of them are spam, but I have a hunch that some are emails from the bullies. It really bothers me when I go online and there are so many emails for me from people I don't know. I'm not sure what to do. Should I open them?

It seems that you have been suffering cyberbullying in silence for a while now, so it's great that you have finally spoken about it and decided to ask for help. First, don't open any of the emails that you think are from the bullies. Put them in a separate folder and keep them as evidence. As well as upsetting you, they could carry a virus or worm. Explain to your family what is happening, and ask them to help you speak to your email provider about what you should do. I think the best thing to do is to change your email account information and give the new information only to those you really trust.

DON'T BE A BYSTANDER

Don't stand by and watch someone being cyberbullied—take a stand and help. Step in, say it's not right, and support the person being targeted. Being cyberbullied makes people feel very alone and frightened. Knowing that someone is on their side will make a huge difference to them.

STOP THIS

If you are online and see nasty messages about someone else, don't join in. Say it's not right to be mean and that it should stop. If you are involved with several conversations at the same time, you might easily ignore someone being cruel or you could even "Like" a hurtful message without thinking, so remember to think before you click.

SPEAK TO THEM

If a friend of yours is a cyberbully, talk to him or her. Don't be aggressive or rude, but discuss how much it must be hurting the victim, and point out that if you allow bullying to go on, someday, it could be you being bullied.

DON'T TAKE PART

Refuse to pass on embarrassing photos that are being sent around the school, and don't laugh at or mock the person being cyberbullied. Let the target know that at least one person is not making fun of them.

If you know someone who is cyberbullying, speak to him or her. Tell them what he or she is doing is wrong, and ask how the cyberbully would feel if he or she became a target.

If you know someone who is being cyberbullied, encourage that person to get help to put a stop to it.

GIVE SUPPORT

If you know someone well who is being cyberbullied, maybe a best friend or a brother or sister, be there for that person. Give him or her your full support, and say lots of positive things to help restore his or her self-esteem. Spend time together doing offline activities. If the cyberbullying gets really bad or is seriously affecting this person, tell an adult you both trust.

Under Pressure Q&A

How can I help my friend?

One of my friends goes to a different school from me. I've noticed she's suddenly started missing a lot of school. I've asked why, and she says she can't face it and that it makes her feel sick. She used to be really funny and happy, but now she looks scared all the time. She nearly always has her phone turned off and won't tell me why, so I think she's being cyberbullied. What can I do to help?

You are being a really good friend. Keep talking to her, and try to get her to confide in you and to speak to an adult at home or at school. She could be feeling so embarrassed and ashamed by what is being said to her, that she doesn't want you or her family to see it. Reassure her that you won't judge her—and that whatever it is that has started the bullying, it is not her fault. Remind her that she has every right to feel safe and happy, and that the first step toward this is to tell an adult about the cyberbullying right now.

DON'T BE A CYBERBULLY

If you are someone who bullies online, think about why you are doing it. Is it to get back at someone because of something that has happened to you? Think what it is like for the person you are bullying. Bullies make their targets feel miserable and worthless, and can cause people to do themselves real harm.

You might think that your bullying is just a joke, or you might be trying to impress your friends, but stop and think about how the person you are bullying is feeling.

CAUSING PAIN

If you are a cyberbully, remember that online actions have real-life consequences. Victims of cyberbullying often become depressed and withdrawn. In extreme cases, they can start self-harming or even try to commit suicide.

SAY YOU'RE SORRY

A good way to end the bullying is to send a message saying it's going to stop and say that you're sorry. If you know the person, apologize face-to-face. He or she may not trust you for a while, but at least this will help to restore some of his or her confidence. Take down any nasty posts you've put up online, and make a promise to yourself not to post anymore, ever.

ASK FOR HELP

Whatever your reason for cyberbullying, there will be adults who will understand. Talk to a school counselor or contact a helpline to get some advice on how you can deal with the feelings that made you cyberbully in the first place.

It's very brave to apologize face to face to the person you've been bullying.

GET POSITIVE

Instead of wasting your time bullying people, use your time online to do something positive and creative. Get involved with a campaign on a site like avaaz.org, or learn a new skill. Or take a break from the online world and do something physical and positive, such as a charity run.

Under Pressure Q&A

They've threatened my brother—what can I do?

My friends are cyberbullying someone and making me join in. I really hate it, but they threatened to start on me and my little brother if I don't go along with it. I really don't want my brother involved—I've seen some of the things they can say and do.

The sooner you break away from this group the better—they're not friends if they're threatening you and your brother. Speak to a teacher at school or a family member, or contact a helpline for advice. Also, tell your brother to let you know if he starts to get any threatening messages and not to feel frightened or embarrassed, whatever they say.

TAKE CONTROL

If you are being cyberbullied, you should do something about it. You do not have to live your life feeling afraid and threatened all the time. There are lots of steps you can take to stop the bullying, but the very first is to believe you have every right to be safe and happy.

ASK FOR HELP

If you are being cyberbullied, tell an adult you trust and who can support you—you need to know you've got someone on your side. Together, you can plan how to handle the situation. Asking for help is the first step to finding a solution.

CALL A HELPLINE

If there is no one you feel you can talk to at school or home, call a helpline. Helpline advisers are specially trained to deal with cyberbullying problems. They can give you practical advice to stop the bullying, as well as advice on how to cope with the negative feelings it causes.

Once you've told someone about the bullying and started a plan to stop it, you'll feel more in control of your own life.

Create a better balance between your online and offline life—spend more time with your family and friends in the real world.

ENJOY YOUR LIFE AGAIN

Most of all, believe that things will get better. Once you have asked for help and taken steps to block, stop, and report the bullies, you can start to enjoy your life again. It's also a really good idea to step away from your devices for a little bit—do more things offline with your friends or family. You can have a life away from your computer and cell phone.

"My online friends gave me the courage to talk"

I felt really ashamed and embarrassed about the messages the cyberbullies were sending me, and I didn't want to talk to anyone about them. I logged on to a helpline and took a look at the message board—the threads were really interesting, so I started one about how I felt. I got lots of really positive and supportive responses, and I didn't feel alone for the first time in ages. It gave me the courage to finally speak to someone, so I went to see the school counselor. She was really understanding and supportive, and finally, I feel that the cyberbullying might soon be over.

YOU ARE NOT ALONE

Being cyberbullied can make you feel as though you are the only person in the world this is happening to, but surveys show bullying happens to a lot of young people. This might not make you feel much better, but at least you know you're not alone and there is a lot you can do about it.

Digital providers take cyberbullying very seriously and will try to help you in any way they can.

PRACTICAL ADVICE

Follow the practical advice in this book about not responding to the cyberbullies, keeping records of the bullying, reporting it, and blocking numbers where you can. No one has the right to bully you, and you have every right to keep yourself feeling safe and happy.

EVERYONE MAKES MISTAKES

Even if you are being cyberbullied for something you've done, such as posting an inappropriate picture or video, no one has the right to make you feel embarrassed or ashamed. Everyone makes mistakes. If this happens, ignore or report the bullies and move on with your life.

SERIOUS STUFF

Most people who are cyberbullied feel too embarrassed or scared to report it or tell an adult. Don't be. Most digital providers have special helpdesks and numbers for reporting malicious or dangerous content online. Although whatever is happening to you might seem really embarrassing and awful, they won't be shocked or judge you.

SPEAK UP

Do not suffer alone. Tell your parents, teacher, or another trusted adult, or go to a helpline. Confide in friends, who will support you if they are true friends. Even if you're not sure who the bully is, tell someone that it is going on, so that you have help dealing with it. There is no need to suffer alone.

"My parents were amazing!"

I sent a friend a personal photo and after we had an argument, she posted it with embarrassing comments. Everyone thought it was hilarious. I hoped it would all blow over, but then I started getting really nasty emails from boys calling me horrible names and sending me disturbing weblinks. I thought that if my parents found out, they'd be furious, but I had to tell someone. I felt sick telling my mom and showing her the picture—how could I have been so stupid? But she was amazing and so was Dad! Mom gave me a big hug and said we'd figure it out. We went to the school and spoke with the principal. He said it was not my fault and that the cyberbullies had to be dealt with. I lost a friend, but I learned a lesson. I'm really pleased I had the courage to tell my parents.

No matter what the cyberbullies are saying or doing to hurt you, people who care for you will understand what you're going through and will want to help you.

GLOSSARY

abusive Insulting, aggressive, and nasty.

anonymous Able to do something—writing a letter, posting a comment, or tweeting, for example—without saying who you are.

antisocial Behaving in a manner that is harmful or annoying to other people or to society in general.

campaign An organized way of working to achieve a set end or goal.

confidential Intended to be kept private or secret.

depression A mental state marked by sadness, inactivity, and lack of self-esteem.

firewall Software that is designed to protect your computer against hackers and viruses.

hacking Breaking into someone else's online accounts illegally.

harassment Annoying or worrying somebody by putting pressure on them or saying or doing unpleasant things to them.

humiliate Make someone feel stupid and ashamed, especially in front of other people.

identity Who you are. A person who uses a false identity is pretending to be someone else.

illegal Against the law.

malicious Intending to be nasty and do harm.

malware Software that is designed and created to cause computer damage and for illegal reasons, such as stealing personal information.

Photoshopped Describing an image having been changed using Photoshop software.

predators People who deliberately target someone to harm or exploit him or her.

procedures Rules and ways of doing things.

provider The company or group that provides an online service such as a web site or chat room.

self-esteem A person's belief in his or her own worth and abilities.

screenshot An image of the display on a computer.

viral Used to describe something that spreads in an uncontrollable way.

viruses Malware that spread from one computer to another by file sharing.

worms Malware that spread from one computer to another, causing damage.

WEB SITES

http://www.childhelp.org
Help and advice about cyberbullying. Includes games, videos, message boards, and chat rooms.

http://www.kidshealth.org/teen
A great web site that covers a wide range of problems faced by young people, including cyberbullying and peer pressure.

http://www.pacer.org/bullying/
The PACER National Bullying Prevention Center web site has lots of advice on cyberbullying and what to do about it.

http://www.nsteens.org
This web site has videos and information to help young people make safe choices online, with advice about cyberbullying.

http://www.stopbullying.gov
A government site that offers practical advice about cyberbullying and how to get help. It also describes the laws on bullying for each state.

HELPLINES

Childhelp 1-800-422-4453 www.childhelp.org.

Samariteens 1-800-252-8336 www.samaritanshope.org

BOOKS

NONFICTION

Cyberbullying by Tracy Brown (Rosen Publishing Group, 2013)

The Bullying Workbook for Teens by Haley Kilpatrick, Raychelle Cassada Lohmann, and Julia V. Taylor (Instant Help, 2013)

Words Wound: Delete Cyberbullying and Make Kindness Go Viral by Sameer Hinduja and Justin W. Patchin (Free Spirit Publishing, 2013)

FICTION

Cyber-Hate: One Act Play by Trisha Sugarek (Create Space Independent Publishing Platform, 2012)

INDEX